The Spy's Guide to Security

BY
Jim Wiese

WITH
H. Keith Melton
SPY EXPERT

SCHOLASTIC INC.

NEW YORK   TORONTO   LONDON   AUCKLAND   SYDNEY
MEXICO CITY   NEW DELHI   HONG KONG   BUENOS AIRES

With the GNOM device shown here, Russian intelligence officers
could have secret, person-to-person communication. The device, developed
during the 1980s, directed the speaker's voice only to the receiver's
headphones. Anyone who was also in the room (without a GNOM device)
would hear only silence, and any bugs planted in the room
would pick up nothing.

ISBN 0-439-33645-7

Copyright © 2003 by Scholastic Inc.

Editor: Andrea Menotti
Designers: Robert Rath, Lee Kaplan
Illustrations: Daniel Aycock
Photos: www.spyimages.net

12 11 10 9 8 7 6 5 4 3   3 4 5 6 7 8/0

Printed in the U.S.A.

First Scholastic printing, March 2003

The publisher has made every effort to ensure that the activities in this book are safe when done as instructed.
Children are encouraged to do their spy activities with willing friends and family members and to respect others'
right to privacy. Adults should provide guidance and supervision whenever the activity requires.

TABLE OF Contents

👓 **This means you'll use your Spy Gear in this activity.**

💻 **This means you can find a related activity on the Spy University web site.**

SAFETY

S o, spy trainee, do you play it safe in your everyday life? Do you lock up your bike when you leave it in a public place? How about making sure you've closed the door tight before you leave home? Is your locker combination top secret? And are your valuables stashed out of sight? Good for you! If you remember to take these everyday precautions, you've got the right instincts for protecting yourself (and your stuff!). Those instincts will come in handy during your spy training!

In the spy world, it's *extra* important that certain things (like information, equipment, and, of course, *secrets*!) don't fall into the wrong hands, where they could do a lot of harm. That's why making sure no one is seeing, finding, or taking your most secret stuff is such a key component of your spy work. And guess what? That's what this month's guide is all about!

TOP SECRET

Warning: Special Clearance Required

SECRET

CONFIDENTIAL

By the time you finish your training in spy security, you'll be equipped with all the skills you need to keep ordinary snoops, trained **counterspies**, and everyone in between from discovering your secrets. You'll learn all about **classifying** secret information, preventing leaks, catching sneaks, and more!

Think you're ready to make your **spy network** more safe and secure? Well, let's not take any chances. Here's some more background information on the world of spy security to get you started.

First

What Exactly Is Spy Security?

"Security" covers just about everything spies do to keep themselves and their secrets safe from others. You've already learned about how to use secret **codes**, **ciphers**, and invisible ink to keep messages from being understood by the wrong people. That's one type of security measure. Here are some others:

- **Using secret hiding places** to protect valuable information and spy equipment.

- **Destroying secret documents** you no longer need so that no one finds them later.

- **Making sure that no one is snooping around** your spy headquarters or following you.

What Can Be Done to Increase Security?

There are many things spies can do to keep themselves and their secrets safe:

- Spies can organize documents at their headquarters (HQ) or **base of operations** so they know what information is classified and must be handled with special care.

SPY EYE PERIMETER ALARM

- Spies can use alarm systems to alert them when someone is trying to sneak into their HQ.

- Spies can use a technique called **trapping** to find out if their materials were searched or if their HQ was entered while they were out.

- Spies can use **danger signals** to make sure that they know immediately when a spy in their network has been nabbed by counterspies.

You'll learn how to master all of these techniques (and many more!) as you work through this month's guide. Remember, you can never go wrong by being overly cautious. A spy is only as good as his first mistake; there may not be a second chance. Keep this in mind as you start your training in spy security!

ABOUT THIS MONTH'S SPY GEAR

We didn't forget to *secure* you some special safety-boosting Spy Gear this month! To help make your **spy network** as safe as can be, you've been issued:

■ **The Spy Eye.** Once this **perimeter** alarm is turned on, you'll know if someone is trying to sneak up on you.

■ **Top Secret Stamper.** You can use this to classify your most valuable information.

ABOUT THIS MONTH'S WEB SITE

You now have access to a whole new section of the Spy University web site at **www.scholastic.com/spy**. You can make some security supplies (like Do Not Enter signs) and you can try your hand at reassembling shredded documents. You can also test your skills at spotting surveillance and keeping your spy work secure. Log on soon!

A word to wise spies

- Don't hesitate to ask for the help of a senior spy (an adult) whenever you need it. We'll remind you when we think it's a good idea!

- Remember: There's safety in numbers! Do your operations with friends and family, and in safe places.

- Always respect the privacy of others when you're on your missions, especially when it comes to surveillance. Since you can never be sure if someone feels comfortable about being watched or followed, ask first. It's always better to be safe than sorry!

the password spot

Shhh. This month's web site password:

safetyrules

SPY TALK

▼ **Base of operations:** A spy's headquarters.

▼ **Burn bag:** A special bag where highly classified documents that are no longer needed are collected for burning (to ensure their complete destruction).

▼ **Cipher:** A form of code in which the letters of a message are replaced with a new set of letters or numbers according to some rule.

▼ **Classified information:** Information available to a limited number of people.

▼ **Classify:** To arrange in categories.

▼ **Code:** A system designed to hide the meaning of a message by substituting letters, numbers, words, symbols, sounds, or signals in place of the actual text.

▼ **Confidential:** The lowest U.S. security classification level for documents and information.

▼ **Counterintelligence:** The protection of information, people, and equipment from spies.

▼ **Counterspy:** Someone who works in counterintelligence, investigating and catching spies.

▼ **Countersurveillance:** Techniques used to detect enemy surveillance.

▼ **Cover:** A false identity or a fake business that spies use as a "front" to conceal their espionage.

▼ **Danger signal:** A prearranged code used by a spy to alert his handlers that he has either been captured or that his cover has been blown. A danger signal can also be sent by the handler to warn the spy.

▼ **Dead drop:** A temporary hiding place used for secret communication and exchange of materials between a spy and a handler.

▼ **Espionage:** The field of spying.

▼ **Forge:** To fake or imitate something (like handwriting) with the goal of making others believe it's real.

▼ **Handler:** An intelligence officer who manages an agent and gives him assignments.

▼ **Microdot:** A tiny photograph of a message, secret document, or other image that can only be read with a magnifier.

▼ **Perimeter:** The outer edge or boundary of an area.

▼ **Secret:** A high U.S. security classification level for documents and information, below Top Secret.

▼ **Security classification:** A rating, like Top Secret, Secret, or Confidential, that indicates exactly how secret or sensitive certain information is.

▼ **Spotter:** A member of a counter-surveillance team who looks out for enemy surveillance.

▼ **Spy network:** A group of spies who work together toward a common goal.

▼ **Surveillance:** The careful study of someone or something.

▼ **Top Secret:** A very high U.S. security classification level for documents and information. (There is a higher classification than Top Secret called SCI, or Special Compartmented Intelligence.)

▼ **Trapping:** A technique used to determine if materials have been touched or if a room has been entered while a spy is away. (When spies set a trap on a door, for example, they say they have "trapped" the door.)

SAVE THE Surprise!

SPYquest

"I'd like to throw a surprise party for Dad's birthday," your mom announces one day after school. "Will you help me plan it?"

Hmmm. Trying to get *anything* past your dad is nearly impossible. Not only does he have super-sharp ears and a keen sense of observation, but he always seems to find out about everything before anyone else. Your mom will definitely need your help with keeping the party under wraps. It'll certainly be worth it to see the look of shock on Dad's face if you succeed!

"Sure," you say. "I'll help."

As the first step, your mom agrees to have a planning meeting (with you and your little sister) on Saturday morning, while Dad's out getting a haircut. You have two locations in mind—your bedroom or the park. Your bedroom is pretty secure, since it's also your spy headquarters, but the park is out of the house completely, where Dad isn't likely to find you.

This is your Spy Quest for this month. Choose your path wisely! If you hit a dead end, you'll have to back up and choose another path!

■ If you decide to have the meeting in your headquarters, turn to **page 12**.

■ If you decide to have the meeting at the park, turn to **page 24**.

Party Plans

TOP SECRET

Happy Birthday

1

OPERATION
HomeBASE

When you play a game of tag, you're always safe when you reach "home base," right? Well, even though the spy world is no game, real spies also need a safe place, which is known as their **base of operations** or headquarters (HQ). There, they can plan their operations, store their secrets, and hide their gear.

How do you make sure that your spy headquarters is safe? A good way to start is to develop a few basic procedures that everyone in your **spy network** will follow. Ready? Set? Then GO ahead and start shaping up security at your home base!

STUFF YOU'LL NEED

- **Notebook**
- **Ruler**
- **Scissors**
- **Thin cardboard**
- **Pencil**
- **Red and green markers**
- **Tape**

YOUR NETWORK

- **A senior spy to help with the scissor work**

WHAT YOU DO

PART 1:
WHO GOES THERE?

The first thing that a base of operations needs is a secure area log. A spy should keep a log of all the people who enter and exit a secure area (like your room).

1 In a notebook, make a chart like the one on the right. It includes columns where you can record the date and time a person enters, his name, signature, and the time of exit in military time. (Check your *Trainee Handbook* for a refresher on military time.)

2 Whenever someone enters the secure area, ask him to fill in the first four columns. When he leaves, fill in his time of departure.

Date	Time Entering	Name	Signature	Time Exiting
March 12, 2003	1135 hrs	Mr. A. Guest	A Guest	1320 hrs

PART 2:
DO NOT ENTER!

Whenever you're in a secret meeting or handling secret information in your HQ, it's good to let others know so they don't enter the room without permission. A DO NOT ENTER sign is one way to do this. Even though a simple sign might not keep out the most determined snoops (we'll let you know how to deal with *them* later!), most people will respect your privacy and come back later.

Note: You can make your sign according to the directions below, or you can design and print one out on the Spy University web site (**www.scholastic.com/spy**).

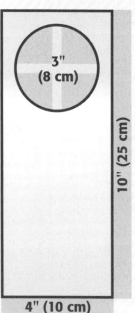

3"
(8 cm)

10" (25 cm)

4" (10 cm)

1 Cut a thin piece of cardboard into a 4x10-inch (10x25-cm) rectangle. The measurements don't have to be exact.

2 Draw a 3-inch (8-cm) circle centered ½ inch (1.5 cm) from the top edge. The circle doesn't need to be exact—you can draw it freehand.

3 Have a senior spy help you cut out the center of the circle by poking the point of the scissors through the cardboard to make a hole. Then cut around the outline of the circle.

4 Write ENTER on one side of the cardboard using the green marker (since green means "go!"). You might also include other messages here, like PROPER SECURITY CLEARANCE REQUIRED.

DO NOT ENTER
Meeting in Progress

DO NOT ENTER
KEEP OUT

DO NOT ENTER
NO Exceptions!

ENTER But Please Knock

ENTER Proper Security Clearance Required

ENTER Be Prepared to Show ID!!

5 Turn the cardboard over and write DO NOT ENTER on the other side using the red marker. You might also add some other messages or warnings, like KEEP OUT.

6 Add other decorations to the sign, like the emblem of your spy network or other simple designs. But don't add too much, or you'll distract people. Your message should be the first thing they notice.

7 To use your sign, hang it on the doorknob to your base

of operations. When it's okay for others to enter, like before a meeting of your spy network starts, turn the sign to the ENTER side. This lets people know that it's okay to come into the room. When the meeting is about to start, turn the sign over so that the DO NOT ENTER side is showing. This will let people know that they shouldn't come in.

PART 3:
NOTE TO SELF

Another helpful security measure is to make a SECURE/NOT SECURE sign. It'll remind you to always lock away secrets.

1 In the spy world, Top Secret information is kept in very secure places, such as a combination safe or a locked box. So, the first thing you need to do is find a locked storage space for your most valuable things. For example, you might keep secret information in a small box with a padlock, or write secrets in a journal that requires a key to open it.

2 Using the pencil and ruler, sketch a 2x3-inch (5x8-cm) rectangle on a piece of thin cardboard. Then cut it out.

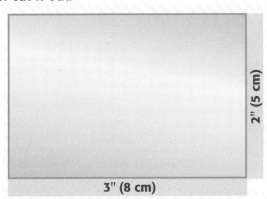

3" (8 cm)

2" (5 cm)

3 Place the cardboard horizontally in front of you and draw a thin pencil line 1 inch (2.5 cm) from the top edge, dividing the rectangle in half.

4 In the top half, write the word SECURE in block letters using the green marker.

5 Rotate the cardboard halfway so that the writing is now on the bottom half, upside down.

SECURE

NOT SECURE

6 In the *new* top half, write the words NOT SECURE in block letters using the red marker.

7 Place a tape loop on the back of the cardboard sign. Your SECURE/NOT SECURE sign is now ready to use.

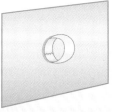

8 You can place the sign on your locked storage container with the SECURE half on top. Whenever you open the container to access your secret information, turn the sign so that the NOT SECURE half is on top. When you're done, return the secret information, lock the container, and turn the sign around so that the SECURE half is on top. The sign will be a constant reminder to secure your most valuable secrets!

MORE FROM HEADQUARTERS

Remember, the Spy University web site (**www.scholastic.com/spy**) is your source for security supplies! Design and print out your own doorknob signs!

WHAT'S THE SECRET?

You just made three devices to improve the security of your base of operations. They're based on techniques that real spies and spy agencies use.

Just as you learned in this operation, real spy organizations use a secure area log to keep track of people entering and exiting their headquarters. Employees must have an ID badge with an electronic code that allows them access to areas of the building based on their level of security clearance. Visitors to the building sign in with a security guard and are given a visitor's ID badge. When they leave the building, they sign out and return the badge. At the end of the day, the secure area log is checked, along with the electronic employee records, to ensure that everyone who

entered the building has also left. If a spy wanted to steal secrets, he might try to enter the building, meet with a person using a **cover**, and then hide in a closet or bathroom until the building closed. He'd then have the whole night to look for secret information. But the secure area log would let security guards know that he was still in the building, and they could begin a search for him.

The ENTER/DO NOT ENTER and SECURE/NOT SECURE signs are simple reminders for you, members of your network, and others about whether a room can be entered and whether valuable secrets and equipment are secure. Careful spies are a lot less likely to be sorry spies!

SPYquest

(continued from page 8 or 24)

You hold the party planning meeting in your headquarters. Of course, you first make sure that your dad has left the house. Then you gather everyone into your room and close the door, leaving a DO NOT ENTER sign outside. As an extra precaution, you place your Spy Eye perimeter alarm on the floor behind you, in case Dad misses your sign and comes inside.

While you're deciding who's going to order the cake, make the invitations, and put together party favors, you hear a knock. Good thing Dad is so respectful of your privacy! You

quickly cover the party information and invite Dad into the room. He doesn't suspect a thing when you tell him that you were just showing everyone your new Spy Eye. He says he's grilling hot dogs for lunch and invites everyone to join him downstairs.

After Dad leaves, you quickly draw the meeting to a close. But before your mom and sister get up to leave, you have to decide what to do with all the party information. You each have a list of the jobs you're supposed to do, and everyone promises to keep the lists

completely out of sight—but you wonder if the best plan would be for you to keep all the information together in your room. It might be safer that way, although that would mean more stuff for you to keep track of and more traffic in your room.

- If you decide everyone can hold on to their job lists themselves, turn to **page 20**.

- If you feel more comfortable holding on to everything, turn to **page 16**.

#2

OPERATION TOP SECRET

Guess what: All secrets are *not* created equal. Some secrets are much more secret than others, so they require *extra* special treatment, lest they fall into the wrong hands! But how can you make sure your **spy network** knows what kind of treatment each secret requires? That's where a **security classification** system comes in handy.

Stuff You'll Need

- **Three file folders**
- **Markers (red, orange, and black)**
- **Top Secret Stamper**

A classification system will help you keep track of all your secrets according to how secret they are. That way, you'll know what type of attention to give your secret information when it comes to hiding it, sharing it, and even getting rid of it when it's time to clean house!

In this operation, you'll divide your secrets into these three security classifications, in order of highest to lowest level of secrecy.

TOP SECRET
SECRET
CONFIDENTIAL

Read on to find out more–and to become a real *classy* spy!

What You Do

Part 1: File in Style

In this part of the operation, you're going to make three different file folders to hold different types of secret documents.

1 Start with a plain folder and use the red marker to draw a series of red diagonal marks along the outer edge of the folder. As you might remember from your *Trainee Handbook*, these markings indicate a Top Secret file folder, which will be used to store your most important and sensitive documents.

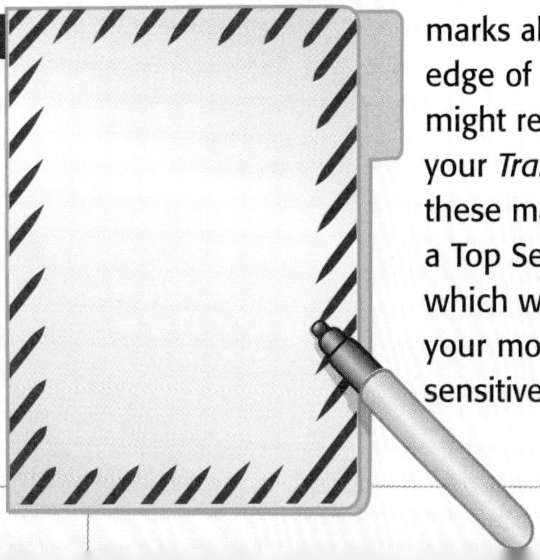

2 Use the red marker to write TOP SECRET in block letters on the front of the folder. Below that you can write other security warnings, such as FOR YOUR EYES ONLY or WARNING: SPECIAL CLEARANCE REQUIRED.

3 Take a second file folder and use the orange marker to put a series of orange diagonal marks along the outer edge of the folder. This will be your Secret file folder.

4 Use the orange marker to write SECRET in block letters on the front of the folder.

5 The third folder is for material that's classified as Confidential. Use the black marker to put a series of black diagonal marks along the outer edge of the folder.

6 Use the black marker to write CONFIDENTIAL in block letters on the front of the folder.

PART 2: A CLASS ACT

Now that you have folders to store your **classified information**, the next step is to decide what to put in each one. Since your folders are based on the U.S. security classification levels for documents, you should think about protecting your secrets in the same manner. The U.S. security system ranks secrets by the amount of damage to national security that would occur if enemy spies got a hold of them.

Here are some examples of file folders used by actual intelligence services. The folders you created are based on these designs.

■ **TOP SECRET** files could cause enormous damage to national security if they got into the wrong hands. Only people who have been investigated for years (and have passed lie detector tests!) have clearance to see them.

■ **SECRET** files could cause serious damage to national security if they were stolen. More people have access to this level of classification than to Top Secret files.

■ **CONFIDENTIAL** files would cause *some* damage to security, but they have fewer restrictions on their use and are seen by the largest number of people.

1 Pick out the most important information you have. This includes secrets that could seriously hurt your spy network if anyone found out about them, such as a list of the hiding places where you've stashed your spy equipment. Put this information in your Top Secret folder. Only *you* should have access to the folder, although you can selectively share the contents with a trusted few on a need-to-know basis.

SPYtales

Even with security classifications, secrets aren't safe if the people who have access to them can't be trusted. The story of Samuel Morrison is one example of this problem.

After Morrison served as a U.S. naval officer during the Vietnam War (1964–1975), he became an analyst at the Naval Intelligence Support Center. With the approval of his Navy superiors, he was also a part-time representative for *Jane's Fighting Ships*, a British magazine that publishes unclassified information about navies from around the world. What Morrison's superiors *didn't* realize was that he would be tempted to abuse his security clearance to steal photos that would be valuable to *Jane's*.

In 1984, Morrison gave in to temptation and stole three secret satellite photos of a Soviet nuclear-powered aircraft carrier

(*Kuznetsov*) as it was being built at a Black Sea shipyard. He then cut the "Secret" labels off the photographs

and sent them to *Jane's*. The satellite photos were published, giving the Soviets insight into the incredible level of detail U.S. spy satellites could provide.

Morrison was soon arrested for stealing and giving away the photos. Although Morrison denied any knowledge of the theft, when the photos were later analyzed, his fingerprint was discovered on one of them. And when the FBI later searched Morrison's home, they found other classified information there. Although Morrison didn't sell the information, he was nonetheless the first person tried and found guilty of a section of the 1917 Espionage Act, which prohibits people from showing classified information to others.

2 Use your Top Secret Stamper to stamp each item in your Top Secret folder, so you'll know exactly how important and private it is, even when it's outside the folder.

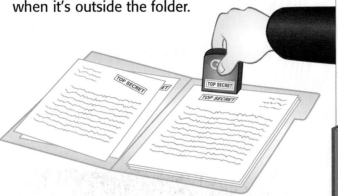

3 Now let's focus on your Secret folder. In this folder, put information that would weaken your network if it got into the wrong hands (but not as seriously as your Top Secret stuff would). This might include the keys to your **codes** and **ciphers**. Only the most trusted members of your network should be allowed to access this information.

4 Put less secret documents into your Confidential folder. These are documents that you still don't want everyone to see, but are okay for your entire spy network to access. This might include notes from your meetings.

5 Your secrets are now filed and organized by level of secrecy. Be sure to keep your folders in a secure location! See **More from Headquarters** for some suggestions.

MORE FROM HEADQUARTERS

Here are some good places to store your folders:

■ **Inside a locked file cabinet or drawer.** Be sure to use your SECURE/NOT SECURE sign from **Operation Home Base**! If you don't have a locked cabinet or drawer, you can try a clever hiding place, like the next two examples.

■ **Inside an old suitcase.** Hide the suitcase in your closet, under other items.

SPYquest

(continued from page 12)

You decide that it's safest to store all the party information in your room, hidden in an old board game box. You classify the party info Top Secret—only you, your mother, and your sister will be able to access it.

After hiding away most of the information, you take out your list of duties and look it over. You're in charge of ordering the cake, picking up balloons, and cleaning up the basement before the party. Suddenly, you remember that your friend Liz's uncle owns a bakery. Maybe her uncle will give you a good deal if you order the cake there, or at least throw in some free cookies for you. It's worth a shot! You know you can certainly trust Liz with a secret. She's a member of your spy network, after all, and you know she'd be happy to help you out. Should you give Liz access to the information, too?

■ If you decide to ask Liz to help you, turn to **page 31**.

■ If you decide to order the cake on your own, turn to **page 40**.

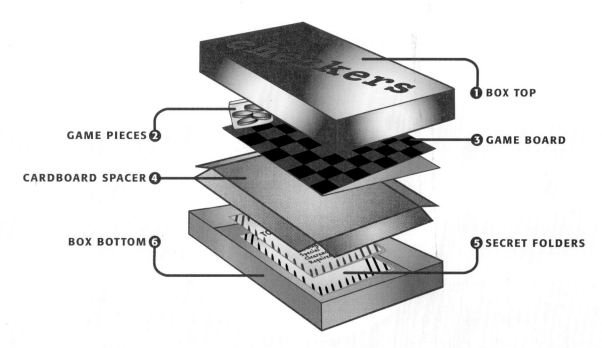

1 BOX TOP

GAME PIECES **2**

3 GAME BOARD

CARDBOARD SPACER **4**

BOX BOTTOM **6**

5 SECRET FOLDERS

■ **Inside an old board game box.** Some board games have a folded cardboard piece in the bottom of the box with a hollow compartment below it (these cardboard pieces are used to hold the game board near the top of the box when you put it away). Remove the cardboard and any game pieces, and place the folders in the bottom of the box. Replace the cardboard, game pieces, and game board, and then put the game away somewhere in your headquarters, out of reach. Even if someone were to discover the game and decide to play it, your folders will still be hidden by the cardboard.

WHAT'S THE SECRET?

All secrets have something in common: They contain information that you don't want everyone in the world to know. But some secrets would cause more harm than others if the wrong people discovered them. Using a classification system helps you and your spy network be as cautious as you need to be.

By dividing up your secrets into Top Secret, Secret, and Confidential folders, you can easily remember who has access to what secrets, how carefully you need to hide them, and how certain you need to be that no one walks in on you while you look at them. Plus, if you had to escape in a hurry, you would know which files to take with you or to destroy first so that enemy **counterspies** couldn't get to them (you'll learn all about destroying documents in **Operation Let 'Er Rip** on the next page).

(continued from page 40)

The next day, you come home from school and put your bag down in the family room. You hear your dad having a conversation in the kitchen.

"What color icing do we want on the cake?" he asks. "What cake? Ohh. . . ."

Oops! You should've known not to leave a phone number with the bakery, or at least you should have told them to make sure they specifically asked for you if they called, just in case your dad answered the phone! That was a critical security error.

■ No cake for you! This was a dead end. Turn back and try again!

17

3

OPERATION LET'ER Rip

When you throw away a note that you don't want anymore, do you simply toss it in the trash, do you crumple it up and then pitch it, or do you rip it into tiny pieces? It probably depends on what the note says, right? Well, spies use the same reasoning when they destroy documents that they no longer need to have around. They take extra care to get rid of their **classified information**, to make sure that no one ever sees it later. One way they do this is to shred the documents into pieces with a machine. Even if the shreds are discovered, they're difficult to put back together. Or *are* they? Try this operation to find out!

STUFF YOU'LL NEED

- **Notebook paper**
- **Pencil**
- **Scissors**
- **Ruler**
- **Tape**

YOUR NETWORK

- **A friend to piece together your shredded messages**

WHAT YOU DO

PART 1: CUT IT OUT

Try this activity to see if shredding classified documents is an effective way of destroying them.

1 Write out a long message to a friend. Make sure that you fill up the page with writing so that you can properly test this shredding method.

2 Now you're going to simulate a shredder's action, using the scissors to cut the paper into thin strips. Begin on one edge of the paper and cut off a ³⁄₈-inch (1-cm) strip of paper.

3 Move in another ³⁄₈ inch (1 cm) and cut another strip of paper.

4 Continue cutting until the entire paper is cut into strips.

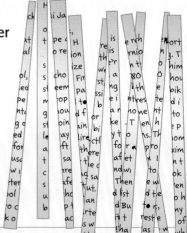

Rose O'Neale Greenhow, a spy for the Confederates (the Southern states) during the American Civil War (1861–1865), learned too late about the importance of destroying unneeded secrets before they caused trouble!

Greenhow was a high-society hostess in Washington, D.C., before the Civil War. She hosted parties for both Southern and Northern politicians, where she let everyone know that she was a Southerner first, last, and always.

When the war began, Greenhow became a Confederate spy. She passed her information, eight messages totaling 1,100 words of text, through a courier to Confederate intelligence. Included were warnings that correctly predicted the Battle of Bull Run. Helped by this information, the Confederates won the battle.

Union intelligence quickly realized that the information that caused their defeat at Bull Run came from Washington. General George McClellan recruited Allan Pinkerton, of the famous Pinkerton Detective Agency, to catch the spy who had given the information to the Confederates. Pinkerton soon zeroed in on Rose Greenhow.

Pinkerton found spy correspondence and reports that Greenhow had stashed throughout her house. In a stove, Pinkerton found unburned letters, and in other places he found little pieces of incriminating documents that had been torn up. These pieces were later reconstructed (like a jigsaw puzzle) so that their contents could be read. They weren't too hard to figure out, because even though Greenhow had used a simple **cipher** issued to her by the Confederates, she had also saved the original versions of her messages. With that information, everything in her eight messages was revealed!

On August 23, 1861, Greenhow was arrested for her activities. She was put in prison and eventually sent south to Richmond, Virginia.

Rose O'Neale Greenhow, shown with her daughter.

5 Mix up the paper strips so they're completely out of order. Then give them to your friend and see if she can put the message back together by matching up the edges of the cut strips and using tape to hold them in place. How does she do?

6 Now have your friend write and shred a long message for *you* to try to put together. How hard is it?

Hi Jack,
Here is the report from my surveillance operation this morning. The target does not appear to realize we're on to him. Good news so far.
First, at 0800 hours, the target walked into school, passing by the bike rack. I noticed that he seemed to be interested in the bikes there. He stopped for a moment to look at a new green mountain bike. Then he proceeded into the school, going directly to Ms. Thompson's classroom. He stayed there for approximately five minutes, then left for the cafeteria. In the cafeteria, he purchased a sausage sandwich, took a bite, grimaced, and threw it out. Then, he went to the back table of the cafeteria and listened to his portable CD player till ... instead of going

PART 2: REST IN PIECES

If strip shredding isn't good enough to protect your secrets from someone skilled at puzzles, then try out this technique.

1 Repeat Part 1 of this operation, but this time, after you've cut the paper into strips, cut the strips into small pieces. This is called a cross-cut.

2 Now have your friend try to put the message back together. How difficult is it *this* time? Could your friend restore the original message? How about you?

MORE FROM HEADQUARTERS

1 Try repeating Part 1 of this operation, but this time, write three different messages on three different pieces of paper. Stack the papers together and cut all three into ⅜-inch (1-cm) strips at the same time. Then try to piece each page back together again. Can you do it this time? What if you used the cross-cutting method? How hard would *that* make it to reassemble the three sheets?

 2 Visit the Spy University web site (**www.scholastic.com/spy**) to test your skills at reassembling shredded documents!

WHAT'S THE SECRET?

As you probably found out in this operation, you can, with a lot of time and effort, piece together a strip-shredded document. You may have been able to find clues to help you, like irregular cuts in the paper, colors of paper and ink, or words that started on one strip and continued on the next. But using these clues becomes more difficult when many pages have been mixed together. And when the paper has been cross-cut into smaller pieces, it becomes almost impossible to piece the message back together.

Still, though, there are even more *surefire* ways to make sure a discarded document won't come back to haunt you. Spy organizations like the CIA use **burn bags** just to be on the safe side. Highly classified documents are put into special bags that are burned in a high-temperature fire to ensure their complete destruction. Taking no chances, the CIA blends the remaining ashes with water and discharges the mixture into the sewer system. Afterward, no one could possibly recover the original documents.

A burn bag used at CIA headquarters.

SPYquest

(continued from page 12)

You decide that it's easiest for everyone to keep their own list of tasks and check things off as they're done. Everyone agrees to store their lists in good hiding places.

Then, one morning a few days later, you find your dad drinking coffee and looking at the newspaper at the kitchen table. As you pour yourself a bowl of cereal, you catch a glimpse of a piece of paper lying in the trash. It's your little sister's slightly crumpled list of jobs for the party! Yikes! She must have thrown her list away when she finished everything. Hoping Dad hasn't noticed the list yet, you quickly grab it and shove it in your pocket. Phew! Dad is still looking down at the newspaper.

"So, Dad, what's new?" you ask casually.

"Oh, not much," he answers with a smile. "I'm just deciding whether to wear my new blue shirt or my green sweater to the party."

■ Drats! You should've known to take extra security precautions with your little sister! This was a dead end. Turn back and try again.

A SHREDDING LESSON FROM IRAN

Intelligence agencies didn't think it was possible to recover documents that had been shredded—until an incident in the late 1970s proved them wrong.

On Sunday, November 4, 1979, a crowd gathered in front of the U.S. embassy in Tehran, Iran. Demonstrations against the United States were so frequent that no one thought it was unusual. But *this* morning was different.

Without any warning, the Iranian demonstrators suddenly swarmed into the compound and surrounded the embassy. The embassy security officer immediately ordered the destruction of secret files, particularly the highly **classified** documents in the communication vault. The communication vault was a small room used to protect classified materials, and, if necessary, destroy them by shredding and burning. Embassy staff quickly began to put classified documents into the shredding machines. Within a few minutes, however, the main shredding machine broke down, so smaller shredders were used instead to continue cutting the papers into thin strips.

Believing that most of the important documents had been destroyed, many of the embassy officials thought they'd protected American secrets. But they were wrong! Many documents remained intact. And even the ones that *had* been shredded didn't discourage the Iranians. They entered the communication vault, collected the mountain of shredded paper, and took it to a large indoor hall where they began sorting through the shreds. Many papers were eventually pieced back together by Iranian women who were skilled at weaving Persian carpets. They were naturals at this task, since their fingers were trained to handle delicate threads.

One of the shredded documents that was reassembled by the Iranians.

In 1982, the Iranians began to publish the classified American documents they'd seized three years earlier. They published *sixty* volumes of information in total! The fact that the Iranians could piece together the shredded documents taught intelligence agencies everywhere a huge lesson, and it changed the security policy for U.S. embassies around the world. Now, improved shredders not only cut paper into strips, but they also cross-cut these strips into small squares of paper. Shredded documents now look more like confetti, instead of spaghetti, and they're virtually impossible to piece back together.

An Iranian postage stamp designed to show that the CIA had been secretly working inside the U.S. embassy.

#4 SoundOff

Imagine this: You've almost finished deciphering a secret message you received when, all of a sudden, you realize your nosy little brother has crept up behind you and read the whole thing! Yikes! Here's a better scenario: You've just opened a file of **Top Secret** information when you hear an alarm go off. You quickly shut the file and hide it under a book, right before your brother walks in. Phew! He didn't see a thing!

STUFF YOU'LL NEED

- 👓 **Spy Eye perimeter alarm**
- **Two AAA-size batteries**
- **Small Phillips screwdriver**

YOUR NETWORK

- **A friend to try to sneak into your base of operations**
- **A senior spy to help with battery installation**

If you liked that second scenario (and don't we all!), then it's time to get your Spy Eye **perimeter** alarm on the job! With your Spy Eye, you'll be able to go about your business at your headquarters without worrying about a younger sibling, an unexpected guest, or even worse, an enemy **counterspy** taking you by surprise!

WHAT YOU DO

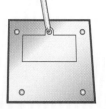

1 With the help of a senior spy, use the screwdriver to open the Spy Eye's battery case, then install the batteries.

2 Set the alarm flat on a table so that the light sensor (the tube sticking out of the side of the device) points off the table.

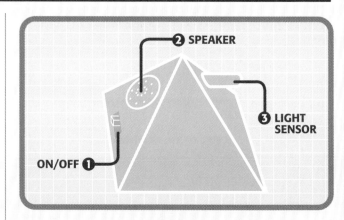

2 SPEAKER

3 LIGHT SENSOR

ON/OFF **1**

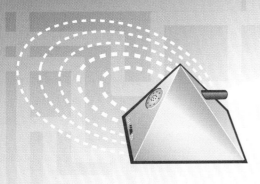

3 Find the ON/OFF switch on the back of the device and turn it to the ON position. Test the alarm by moving your hand in front of the (invisible) alarm beam.

4 Look around your **base of operations**. If someone were going to try to sneak in, where would he most likely enter? The door or a window would be the most obvious ways.

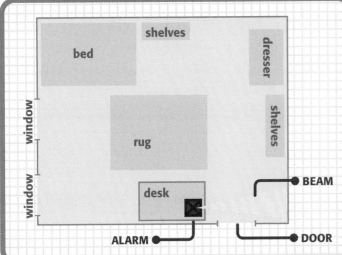

5 Place the Spy Eye so that the alarm beam points across the path an intruder would most likely take. The alarm is light-sensitive—it goes off when it detects changes in light. For this reason, it's best to use the alarm in bright light conditions. If you place the alarm in a dark room, it will go off when the lights are turned on.

6 Turn the alarm on and your perimeter is secure. Your Spy Eye will let you know when someone is trying to sneak up on you.

7 Have some friends try to sneak into your base of operations. See if they set off the alarm, or if they can find a way to avoid getting caught.

8 Turn off the alarm when you're not using it to preserve the batteries.

MORE FROM HEADQUARTERS

1 Try setting the Spy Eye at different heights. For example, try setting it flat on the floor, then on top of a desk. Does the alarm work better when it's on the floor or higher up? How might someone sneak past the alarm when it's in each of those positions?

2 Have your friend set up the Spy Eye, and *you* try to sneak into the base. Does the Spy Eye catch you every time?

WHAT'S THE SECRET?

There are various ways that perimeter alarms like your Spy Eye can be activated. Some alarms are triggered by motion. Others use infrared (invisible light) sensors that are set off by the smallest amount of heat and can detect the warmth of a human body. The sensor in your Spy Eye detects changes in the amount of light that enters into it. In a lit room, there is a certain amount of light that is reflected into the alarm beam. When a person walks in front of the beam, the amount of light reflected into the beam changes. The sensor then completes an electric circuit and the alarm sounds for seven to eight seconds.

If the alarm was placed on the floor and an intruder knew about it, he might just step high over the beam. If the alarm was set higher, an intruder could crawl under its beam. That's the reason why most security perimeter alarms use several detectors to cover all areas.

(continued from page 8)

You decide to have the meeting at the park, but it takes a while for everyone to get ready. Finally, just as you're all leaving the house, who do you see but Dad, pulling into the driveway with his new haircut.

"Where are you all headed?" he asks.

"Just to the park," your mother says.

"Can I come along?" Dad asks.

What a disaster! You really need to start planning for this party, since it's only a week away!

You have to decide what to do: Either let your dad join you and postpone the meeting, or try to discourage him from coming to the park.

- If you decide to postpone the meeting and hold it in your headquarters later on, turn to **page 12**.
- If you try to discourage your dad from coming to the park, turn to **page 26**.

OPERATION
Goldilocks

You know the tale of *Goldilocks and the Three Bears*, right? A little girl goes into the home of a bear family while they're out, gobbles up their porridge, and falls asleep on a bed, only to be found later by the baby bear. Well, let's say Goldilocks had come into *your* room while you were out. Would you be able to figure it out? Probably! But that's because Goldilocks leaves behind some pretty big clues, like empty bowls and rumpled bedspreads. In the real world, most snoops aren't so careless, and, in fact, some can be downright undetectable. Want to know if even the sneakiest "Goldilocks" has been trespassing in *your* **base of operations**? Then try this clever spy technique, named after our fairy-tale friend!

STUFF YOU'LL NEED
- **Toothpick**

YOUR NETWORK
- **A friend to sneak into your base of operations**

WHAT YOU DO

1 Hold one end of the toothpick in one hand, and start to close the door with the other.

2 As you close the door, put the toothpick between the door and the doorjamb. The end that you're holding should stick out from between the door and the doorjamb.

3 Pull the door completely closed.

4 Break off the part of the toothpick that's sticking out of the door by pushing it left and right. The remainder of the toothpick will stay stuck between the door and the doorjamb. Save the piece of toothpick you've broken off. It's now safe to leave your base because you have a Goldilocks alarm in place.

5 When you return to your base, if the piece of toothpick that was between the door and doorjamb has fallen to the floor, you'll know that someone entered the room.

SNAP!

MORE FROM HEADQUARTERS

Another door alarm can be made using a human hair. First, close the door to your base. Next, find a hair that's about 3 inches (8 cm) long (it'll be less noticeable—and a true *Goldilocks* alarm—if it's a blond hair). Wet the hair with saliva and place it so that it runs from the door to the doorjamb about one foot up from the floor (that is, down low so it won't be noticed). The saliva will stick the hair to the door and doorjamb. If someone opens the door, the hair will come unstuck and fall to the floor. When you return, all you have to do is check if the hair is still in place to know whether anyone has entered the room.

HAIR

WHAT'S THE SECRET?

Alarm systems don't have to be complicated or high-tech: A simple toothpick or a single strand of hair can let you know if anyone has been in your base while you were away. This is a technique spies call **trapping**, since a snooper will get caught by the trap (unknowingly) while trying to sneak into your room.

With the toothpick technique, most intruders won't notice something so small and light falling to the ground when they open the door. Even if they *do* see the toothpick and realize it's an alarm, they'll struggle to reset it. They won't be able to wedge the toothpick half back between the door and the doorjamb, and if they try to break *another* toothpick in the door, they won't be able to break it in exactly the same way yours was broken (because no two toothpicks will break alike!). If you're unable to match the half in the door to the other half of your original toothpick, you'll know that a new toothpick has been used. That's why you're supposed to save the broken-off piece!

Similarly, since a hair across the door and doorjamb is so thin and light, it probably won't be noticed by anyone opening the door. You can easily check for the hair when you come back to your room. If it's not there, you've got an intruder alert on your hands!

SPYquest

(continued from page 24)

"Uh, Dad, don't you need to... clean out the car?" you say, remembering your dad mentioned that earlier.

"I can do that later," your dad says.

"Isn't there a game you want to watch on TV?" suggests your sister.

"Not till tomorrow," your dad says.

"Why don't you make lunch so it's ready when we get back?" your mom suggests.

Your dad looks at you all with raised eyebrows.

"Either I'm very unpopular these days," he says, "or this has something to do with my *birthday*...."

Your father looks at the stunned expressions on your faces and smiles.

"I knew it!" your dad says. "But don't cancel the party. I'll still pretend to be surprised!"

■ Too bad! This is a dead end. Turn back and try again!

Give an INCH

Aha! You've figured out that someone entered your **base of operations** while you were away by using the tricks you learned in **Operation Goldilocks**. But now comes the big question: How do you know whether that person was really trying to snoop or just dropping by to visit? And if you *do* have a snooper on your hands, how will you know if your hidden secrets were discovered? You can set traps, that's how—and not the kind that catch mice with a loud *snap*, but the kind that silently catch snoopers without them even knowing it! With the **trapping** technique you'll learn in this operation, you'll find out if your security measures up!

WHAT YOU DO

PART 1: SET THE TRAP!

1 To begin, create a pretend **Top Secret** message. Put a Top Secret stamp on it, so it'll be clear to your friend (who'll be searching for it in Part 2) that this is the message she's supposed to find.

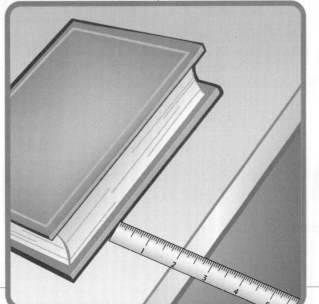

2 Fold the message and place it inside the pages of one of your books.

3 To set a trap using the book, simply place the book on your desk in an exact location. For example, you could use the ruler to place the book exactly 2 inches (5 cm) from the edge of the desk.

4 Place other books on top of and around the original book, being careful not to move it.

5 If you leave your room and return later, all you need to do is measure the distance from the edge of the desk to the book with the message. If someone picked the book up and returned it to the desk, it's unlikely she would have replaced it in *exactly* the same spot.

PART 2: TEST THE TRAP!

Now you're going to have a friend try to find the Top Secret message in your headquarters—*without* setting off your trap!

1 Leave the room and give your friend ten minutes to search. Tell her that she should leave the room exactly as she found it, just like **counterspies** would. Her challenge is to find the Top Secret message without leaving any evidence that she was snooping around.

2 After your friend has finished her search, enter the room (without asking your friend if she found the message) and measure how far the book with the message is from the edge of the desk. If the book's placement has changed at all, you can tell your friend that she was caught by your trap (and explain how). Even if your friend managed to find the message, she aroused your suspicion, so she lost the challenge (and you won!).

3 If the book is in *exactly* the right place, then find out if your friend found the message, or if she searched the book at all. If she did, then your trap was foiled! But don't give up on it. Check out **More from Headquarters** for one way of improving this trapping technique.

MORE FROM HEADQUARTERS

You can be even surer that no one has handled an object in your absence by taking *several* measurements to mark its placement. For example, a book could be 2 inches (5 cm) from the edge of the desk on the right, 3½ inches (9 cm) from the bottom, and 6 inches (15 cm) from the top. Write down all of the measurements and keep them with you so you don't forget them.

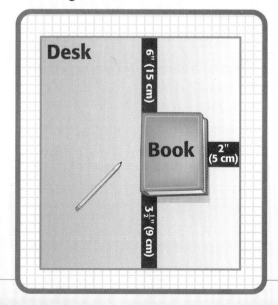

Powder power

You can also use baby powder as a way of detecting if something was touched while you were gone. Just put a small spoonful of baby powder in your hand and blow it over an item (like a book) you want to protect. If someone touches the item, the powder will be disturbed. You'll be able to see finger marks and other smeared or smudged areas in the powder coating. Chalk dust also works for this purpose.

WHAT'S THE SECRET?

By measuring *exactly* where you place an item, you're setting a trap that snoopers can't detect. They'll try to be sneaky, but they just won't be able to *measure up*!

This kind of trap works not only with items on a desk, but also with a picture hanging over a safe on a wall. If you deliberately slant the picture at a particular angle, a snooper would have a hard time hanging it back exactly the right way (and would most likely try to hang it straight!).

SPYquest

(continued from page 40)

You decide to call the bakery back later on so that you don't leave a phone number and risk someone getting a hold of your dad. In the meantime, you and your mom go over the plan for bringing your dad into the house on the day of the party. Here's the plan your mom suggests: On Friday, your dad will pick you up after your soccer practice and take you shopping for new shoes. When you come home in time for dinner at seven and walk through the front door, Dad will be greeted by friends and family waiting in the house.

"Sounds like a plan," you say.

But then it hits you—there should be a danger signal in case something goes wrong.

"If there's a problem, like if Dad wants to come home early or something, I'll call you and say, 'I'm starving! What's for dinner?'"

"Okay," your mom agrees. "But let's try not to let there be a problem."

Friday finally arrives. You finish practice, and Dad is waiting for you according to plan. But when you get in the car, he tells you that he needs to take you home *first* before going shopping because he forgot his wallet there. You have to act quickly, because if you get home too early, your father will see the guests arriving.

You have to decide: You can try to call your mom and give her the danger signal you agreed upon earlier, or you can try to stall your dad yourself so that you'll get home on schedule and not disrupt the plans.

■ If you decide to call your mom with the danger signal, turn to **page 43**.

■ If you try to stall your dad and get home later, turn to **page 38**.

In this operation, you'll really have to use your head—the *hair* on your head, that is. As you learned in **Operation Goldilocks**, hair is a great spy security tool. This operation will show you yet *another* hair-raising snooper trap that'll help you keep tabs on your secrets while you're away from your HQ. Read on to *hair* all about it!

STUFF YOU'LL NEED

- **Pencil and paper**
- **Top Secret Stamper**
- **Book**
- **Strands of hair**

YOUR NETWORK

- **A friend to test your trap**

WHAT YOU DO
PART 1:
SET THE TRAP!

1 Write a pretend **Top Secret** message. Put a Top Secret stamp on it so your friend (who will look for it in Part 2) knows it's the message he's supposed to find.

2 Place the message inside a book.

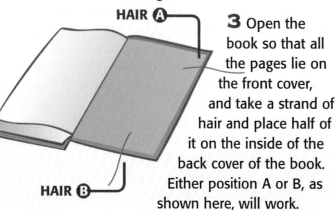

HAIR **A**

HAIR **B**

3 Open the book so that all the pages lie on the front cover, and take a strand of hair and place half of it on the inside of the back cover of the book. Either position A or B, as shown here, will work.

4 Flip over the pages of the book so the hair is held between the last page and the back cover. Then (with the hair in either position A or B) wrap the other half of the hair around the front of the book and tuck it between the front page and front cover of the book. It will help if you hold the book vertically when you do this, so the hair falls easily into place.

Hair Today, Gone Tomorrow

B HAIR **A**

5 Place the book on a table or desk in your headquarters. If the hair is no longer in place when you check for it later, you'll know that the book was opened in your absence.

PART 2:
TEST THE TRAP!

Just like you did previously in **Operation Give an Inch**, you're going to challenge a friend to find your Top Secret message without getting caught by your trap. See which of the two trapping techniques does a better job of catching a snooper!

1 Leave your HQ. Have your friend search the room for ten minutes to try to find the Top Secret message. He should try to put everything back where he found it and leave no trace of his search.

2 After ten minutes, have your friend call you into the room, but don't have him tell you whether he found the message.

A word to wise spies

If your hair is really short, find a shaggier spy to loan you some locks! You can also try experimenting with very fine threads.

3 Check the book. If the hair is no longer in place, then your friend has opened the book and probably found the message. Tell him he was caught by your trap (and explain how). Even if your friend managed to get his hands on your message, he alerted you to his presence, so you have won the challenge!

4 If the hair is still in place, ask your friend if he found the message or searched the book at all. If he did, find out if (and how) he noticed the hair and replaced it. This feedback will help you improve your trapping technique!

MORE FROM HEADQUARTERS

How else could you use a strand of hair as a trap? Consider these ideas:

■ Place a hair on top of a box holding your secret information or Spy Gear. If someone lifts the lid, the hair will fall off. (Only set this trap in a place where the air is still, or a breeze might cause a false alarm!)

HAIR

■ Put a small piece of hair inside a folded note or piece of paper. If someone unfolds the note to read it, the hair will fall out. If the hair is small enough, the snoop won't notice it.

WHAT'S THE SECRET?

It's very unlikely that someone looking through your books, files, or boxes will notice a hair. And even if he does, he probably won't realize that the hair was placed there as a trap! The lightest-colored hairs work best for this technique.

SPYquest

(continued from page 16)

You head over to Liz's house, tell her about the party for your dad, and ask her about the bakery.

"I'm sorry," she says. "My uncle sold the bakery last month. But I can help you look around for another place if you like."

You're in the process of telling her thanks anyway when Liz's mom walks into the room and overhears you.

"Oh, darling, I just love surprises!" she says.

Uh-oh! You know about Liz's mom's reputation for telling everyone about everything. You beg her not to tell anyone about the party, but you have a bad feeling about it all.

Sure enough, before you know it, even your teacher is asking you how the party preparations are coming along. It won't be long before Dad finds out about it, too.

■ You let too many people in on your secrets! This was a dead end. Turn back and try again!

OPERATION

SHAKE it UP

#8

In the last three operations, you learned some **trapping** techniques for doors, for items on a desk, and for secrets tucked inside books. But what if you had some important stuff stored in your backpack? If you had to leave the backpack alone somewhere, how could you find out if it had been searched while you were gone? By trapping it, of course! This operation will show you one way to find out if someone is trying to *shake up* your security when you're not looking!

WHAT YOU DO

PART 1: SET THE TRAP!

1 Take the first canister, and use one marker to put a small colored dot on its lid. Make the dot large enough so you can easily see it, but small enough that it won't draw attention.

2 Use a different colored marker to make a dot on top of each of the other three canisters.

Note: You can also use four different small stickers to mark the tops of the canisters.

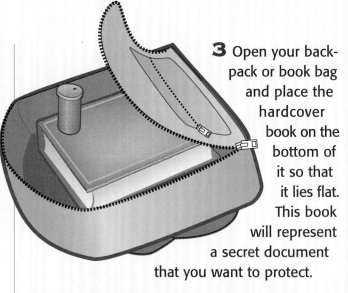

3 Open your backpack or book bag and place the hardcover book on the bottom of it so that it lies flat. This book will represent a secret document that you want to protect.

4 Carefully place one film canister on the book. Take note of the color of the dot (or the design of the sticker) on the canister.

5 Arrange the remaining three canisters in a pattern, such as a line or a square. Make a note of the position of each canister, based on the dots or stickers.

6 Carefully close the backpack or bag, being careful not to shift the canisters. Your trap is now ready to catch a snoop!

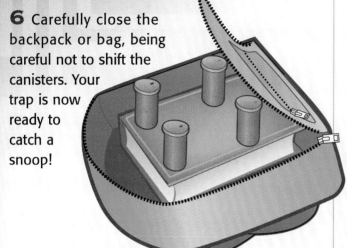

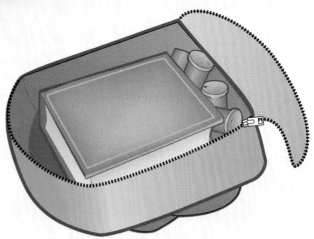

PART 2: TEST THE TRAP!

Just as you did in **Operation Give an Inch** and **Operation Hair Brain**, you're going to put your trap to the test by challenging a friend to search an area without leaving a trace.

1 Have a friend search the room where you've left the bag, looking for the "secret document" (the book). Tell her the title of the book so she knows what she's looking for. Also remind her that she should act like a **counterspy** and try to leave the room exactly as it was. She should not give you any reason to suspect that the room was searched.

2 After your friend has finished searching, go back into the room. You can tell if she searched the backpack by carefully opening the top and looking at the canisters. If your friend lifted the bag to open it, or stuck her hand inside, the canisters will have moved.

3 If the canisters have moved, tell your friend she was snagged by your trap! Even if she *did*

find the book, she *didn't* manage to avoid alerting you. However, if she did somehow search the bag without setting off the trap, make sure to find out how she did that. This feedback will help you improve your technique.

MORE FROM HEADQUARTERS

Instead of using colored dots, try putting a different coin in the bottom of each film canister. For example, you could put a penny in one canister, a nickel in another, a dime in the third, and a quarter in the last. Arrange the canisters in a particular order, remembering which coin is inside each one. To check the trap after your friend has searched your room, open each canister to see which coin's inside.

WHAT'S THE SECRET?

It's difficult for a counterspy, or anyone looking through your stuff, to open a backpack or briefcase without disturbing the canisters. Even if the counterspy guessed that the canisters were arranged in a pattern and attempted to put them back, it's extremely unlikely that she'd get them in the right order. With four different colored dots, there would be twenty-four possible arrangements, and only one would be correct. Any of the other twenty-three combinations would tell you that the bag had been checked.

9

OPERATION write on

I n the spy world, **forging** documents and signatures is a pretty common practice, since spies often have to pretend they're someone else. But a forgery might also be used to trick a spy, and that's where you have to be careful.

Sometimes after **counterspies** penetrate a **spy network**, they'll create phony messages from a trusted person to trick members of the network into meeting them. When the members of the spy network arrive, counterspies are waiting to nab them!

Not ready to be nabbed? Then it's time to learn how to analyze handwritten messages to make sure they're really from the person you think wrote them.

STUFF YOU'LL NEED
- **Pencil and paper**

YOUR NETWORK
- **Four friends to write or forge messages**

WHAT YOU DO

PART 1: WRITE THIS WAY

In this part of the operation, you'll collect and analyze a handwriting sample from a friend. Later, you'll have to pick out his true handwriting from a bunch of forgeries, so pay close attention!

1 Have your friend write you a message. The message should be handwritten (not printed) and at least twenty-five words long to give you

a sizeable sample. For example, you can have your friend write:

You've been doing a good job working for our spy network. Prepare for your next operation later in the week. Be careful, because I think counterspies may be on to us.

Jason

2 Look at each word in the message. Does your friend's writing have any distinct characteristics that would help you recognize it again? For example, there are many things that you can look for in the writing (see below). Try to recognize your friend's handwriting by looking for several of these writing characteristics. To help you, circle things that are distinctive to the handwriting and make a list of them for future reference.

Flying start (Upward stroke) **Downward stroke**

Be or *Be*

FLYING START Where and how does your friend start the first letter of each word? For example, does the **B** in "Be careful" start with an upward stroke or a downward stroke?

Exact retrace **Loose retrace**

a or *a*

d or *d*

RETRACE How are letters that use a retrace (like **a** or **d**) formed? Does the retrace follow the original line exactly?

e or *l*

Rounded e **Narrow e**

LOOPS How are loops formed? Are they rounded or narrow? For example, look at the letter **e**. Is it rounded? Or is it so narrow that it almost looks like the letter **i**?

UPSTROKES How far do letters like **t**, **b**, or **d** extend upward? Are they tall or short?

at or *at*

Tall t **Short t**

Low dot **High dot**

it or *it*

Low bar **High bar**

LIFTS When a letter takes a second stroke to complete it, such as the bar for the letter **t** or the dot for the letter **i**, where is the second stroke placed? Is it placed low or high in relation to the other parts of the letter?

Level **Dip**

op or *op*

an or *an*

Connected **Disconnected**

CONNECTORS How are letters connected to one another? Are there breaks between certain letters?

Quick stop **Flying stop**

doing or *doing*

FLYING STOP How does the last letter in a word end? Does it stop quickly or flow on?

Close letters **Spaced letters**

SPACING How far apart are the letters in a word or the words in the message? Are they close together or far apart?

good or *good*

PART 2:
SPOT THE FORGERIES

Now you're going to test your ability to pick out a real message from your friend from among some forgeries. Let's pretend that the friend whose handwriting you just analyzed is your **handler**, and that counterspies are trying to trick you with fake messages from him. Can you determine which note is really from your handler?

1 While you're out of the room, have the same friend whose sample you analyzed in Part 1 write a second, shorter message on a new piece of paper. For example, he could write:

2 Have your other three friends try to make exact copies of the message, each on a separate piece of paper.

3 Have one person write a number (1 through 4) on the bottom of each message, assigning a different number to each friend. This will help you keep track of who wrote which message.

4 When you return to the room, compare the writing of the four new messages to the writing in the original message from your handler. Begin by looking at how the letters are formed. Do they seem smooth or jerky? The letters in a forgery will often seem jerky since the forger's pen will stop and start while he's trying to copy someone else's writing.

5 Next, look at the individual characteristics of the writing. Do you recognize any of the unique characteristics of your handler's writing? For example, look at the loops, retraces, flying starts, spacing, and letter formation for the same words in both messages. Where are they the same and where are they different? Take a look at your notes from Part 1 to see if the forger might have missed an element of the writing style of your handler. Can you pick out which message is from your handler and which ones are forgeries?

Our next secret meeting will be tomorrow after school by the frog pond.

Our next secret meeting will be tomorrow after school by the frog pond.

WHAT'S THE SECRET?

Believe it or not, your handwriting changes slightly each time you write. Why? It may change due to your physical and emotional state (like whether you're excited, sleepy, or nervous); or it may change because you're in a hurry, or if you're trying to write while you're on the move! However, the shape of the letters and the way certain letters are formed and joined will stay mostly the same. These characteristics can be used to spot a forgery—if the *write* analysis is used! Some people believe that handwriting can tell you a lot about the writer's personality. For instance, if someone doesn't dot all his **i**'s or cross all his **t**'s, he might be absentminded. If someone's writing slants to the right, she might be a positive thinker. What does your writing say about you?

10

OPERATION Tailspin

Even if your **base of operations** is in pretty good shape security-wise, how safe are *you* when you leave it? Another important aspect of security is being able to detect and escape enemy **surveillance**. Spies have to be certain that no one is watching or following them while they go about their missions, attend meetings, and access their **dead drops**. And if **counterspies** *are* watching, spies need to know about it, so they can avoid or escape surveillance whenever necessary. Try this operation to learn how.

STUFF YOU'LL NEED
- **Notebooks**
- **Pencils**

YOUR NETWORK
- **A friend to play the role of a counterspy**

WHAT YOU DO

1 Have a friend try to follow you several times during the next week, in safe places such as on your way to and from school or even *during* school at recess. Your friend should keep his plans to follow you a secret, but keep a journal of the days and times he actually follows you.

2 Go about your activities for the week, keeping your own journal of the times you see your friend following you. Try to find and even lose the surveillance with these tips:

■ **Be aware of your surroundings.** Observe what is happening each day as you go about your daily activities. For example, are there certain people you usually see on your way to school?

■ **Switch directions several times when walking.** Try doubling back on your path, pretending you forgot something. This will allow you to check whether anyone is following you.

■ **Try checking a reflection.** If you walk up to a large store window, you can use the reflection to check what's going on behind you without turning around.

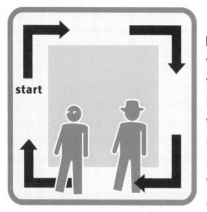

■ **Go around the block, making four right turns in a row.** When you go around each corner, take note of who is on the same street as you. The four turns will get you back on the street where you started. If you see the same person behind you after all those turns, he is probably following you.

3 At the end of the week, compare journals with your friend. Were you able to detect him every time he followed you? How many times did he go undetected?

MORE FROM HEADQUARTERS

 Stop by the Spy University web site (**www.scholastic.com/spy**) for another surveillance-spotting challenge. See if you can detect the counterspy who's following you!

WHAT'S THE SECRET?

The best way to detect surveillance is to be aware of your surroundings at all times—*without* being obvious. And whenever you think you're being tailed, it's important to continue your normal actions, and not suddenly run away. A counterspy may only *suspect* that you're a spy. If you run away, he will know for sure that you're trying to hide something.

Sometimes spies just *let* counterspies follow them around—if they're not doing any spy work, it's better not to alarm the counterspies by giving them the slip. But spies *do* need to figure out ways to get away from surveillance for short periods (sometimes only a minute or two), like when they need to use a dead drop to exchange information. Dead drops are ideally located in places that are out of view but easily accessible, like in parks, behind trees, under bridges, or in restrooms. If the spy transfers information very quickly, while out of view only for a moment, those tailing him are not likely to get suspicious.

(continued from page 29)

You decide to stall your dad so your mom has time to get all the guests into the house and doesn't have to worry about you arriving too early. First you ask your dad if he wants to kick the soccer ball around with you, but he says he's in a hurry to get home. You then spend an extra long time getting your stuff together, but Dad starts to help you out and hurry you along, saying that the store will close. As a last resort, you say that you need to use the restroom before the drive home. You spend a really long time in there.

"What in the *world* took you so long?" your dad asks.

"Just...the usual," you say sheepishly.

"I've never known you to take that long in the restroom," your father says, looking suspicious. "Are you *stalling*, by any chance?"

"No," you say, trying to look innocent. "I just...took a while."

"Call me crazy," he says, "but I get the feeling that something's going on here. People have been acting funny all week. Does this have anything to do with my *birthday*?"

Dad quickly spots the alarm in your eyes.

"You don't have to say," he says. "I'm sure I'll be *surprised* when I find out!"

■ Too bad! That was a dead end, all right. Turn back and try again!

OPERATION DOUBLE Team

Y ou've always been taught that it's safer to travel in groups, right? Well, the same rule applies in the spy world when it comes to dealing with **surveillance**. Surveillance teams are made up of **counterspies** operating together to watch and follow spies (which makes it much more difficult for spies trying to spot a tail). But two can play at that game! Spies assemble their own **countersurveillance** teams, with members of their **spy network**, and work together to see if they're being followed. See how the match up of the two teams plays out!

STUFF YOU'LL NEED

- **Notebooks**
- **Pencils**

YOUR NETWORK

- **Several friends to act as a surveillance team, and another friend to help you detect their surveillance**

WHAT YOU DO

1 Ask a friend to appoint two other friends to be the counterspies on a surveillance team that's in charge of following you. Tell your friend not to tell you who these people are.

2 Ask another friend to work with you as your **spotter** (to help you *spot* the surveillance team).

3 Have the surveillance team try to follow you during the next two days. They can follow you in safe places, such as on the way to school or even while you're at school. They should keep a journal of the different things they see you doing.

4 For the next two days, go about your normal activities, and try to figure out who's on the surveillance team that's following you.

To help you detect the surveillance, your spotter should accompany you whenever possible. Your spotter should follow about thirty paces behind you, or across the street. His only job is to look for people who are following you. You should keep a record in your notebook of each time you or your spotter think you've noticed the surveillance team.

5 At the end of the second day, have the friend who appointed the surveillance team reveal who was on it. Did you guess correctly?

6 Next, compare the surveillance team's records with yours. Was the surveillance team able to follow you without you or your spotter noticing, or did you spot the counterspies every time?

MORE FROM HEADQUARTERS

A surveillance team may also be on the lookout for a spotter when they're tailing a spy. To prevent them from realizing you've got a spotter on the watch, have your spotter use quick-change disguises (putting on new hats, jackets, and so on) in order to throw off the surveillance team.

(continued from page 16)

You decide to call the bakery yourself to be on the safe side. Maybe if you mention knowing Liz, you'll still get your free cookies! When someone answers the phone, you start to explain what you need.

"Well, I don't usually handle cake orders," the person on the other end says. "But I can write down what you need and have the baker call you back if she has any questions."

You wonder what to do, because you really need to make sure the cake order goes in today so it'll be ready in time.

- If you decide to leave a message, turn to **page 17**.
- If you decide to call back later, turn to **page 29**.

Wise spies always say...

- If you see an unknown person once, it's interesting.

- If you see that person twice, it's a coincidence.

- If you see that person three times, it's enemy surveillance!

WHAT'S THE SECRET?

A team approach will help you detect surveillance better than you could if you were working alone. You used *one* spotter, but real spies will often use several spotters to keep an eye out for enemy counterspies.

Spies also have other techniques to outwit surveillance teams. For one, they'll set up daily *routines*. They'll take the same route to work, eat at the same restaurants, jog on the same paths, and so on. These routines can work to the spy's advantage, since the surveillance team will start to feel like everything's under control, and that there's nothing to be suspicious about. If the counterspies think they can safely predict where the spy will be at any given time, they may relax their tight surveillance. This gives the spy some room to operate undetected!

Signal

DANGER

#12

There are times when all the security measures in the world aren't enough, or when spies simply get sloppy and are captured by **counterspies**. That might sound like the *end* of the spy tale to you, but it may actually be the time for spies to do the most important part of their job: protecting the rest of their **spy network**. If captured, a spy always has her last line of defense, the **danger signal**.

A danger signal is not a loud alarm or a bunch of red flares. Nothing like that. Rather, it's a secret signal that a captured spy can use if she's being forced to help counterspies trap other spies. For example, if the counterspies make the captive spy send messages to her network to invite them to a meeting where the counterspies will try to catch them, the spy can include a secret danger signal in the message to let the network know there's trouble, and that they shouldn't come to the meeting.

Try this operation to learn how to create a danger signal (although we hope you'll never need it!).

STUFF YOU'LL NEED
● **Pencil and paper**

YOUR NETWORK
● **A friend to receive your messages**

DANGER!

WHAT YOU DO

1 Work with the members of your network to decide on a danger signal. Here are some ideas:

■ **Deliberately misspell a certain word.** For example, if the third word of a message is misspelled, it could mean there's danger, and that the message should not be believed.

Please be carefull on your way to sc... forget that tonight or tomorrow...

41

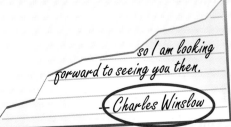

so I am looking forward to seeing you then.

—Charles Winslow

■ **Sign the message with a certain cover name.**

For example, when the message is signed with the name "Charles Winslow," it could mean that the spy has been caught.

will let you know as soon as I can!

—J. W.

■ **Sign the message with initials instead of**

a full name. Ending the message "J.W." instead of "Jim Wiese" could mean there's trouble.

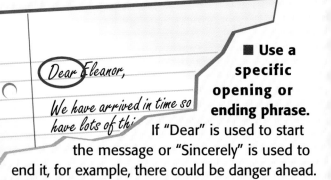

Dear Eleanor,

We have arrived in time so have lots of thi—

■ **Use a specific opening or ending phrase.**

If "Dear" is used to start the message or "Sincerely" is used to end it, for example, there could be danger ahead.

SPYtales

Velvalee Dickinson was a Japanese spy who worked in the United States during World War II (1939–1945). Because of a lifelong interest, she opened a shop in New York that sold dolls, toys, and antiques. Her store was very successful, and she was soon selling her goods across the United States and around the world. Her business also gave her the perfect cover for seeking and sending secret information.

Velvalee used "business" trips to the West Coast to spy on naval shipyard activity in San Diego and San Francisco. She also used her dolls as a **code** to send messages to her Japanese **handlers**. For example, when she wrote, "I have just received a doll with a hula skirt," in a letter it would really mean that a naval warship just arrived in San Diego from Hawaii.

To increase her security, Velvalee sent all her messages to Japan through a contact in Buenos Aires, Argentina. She would also use the return addresses of her women clients on the letters to hide her identity. It seemed like a great plan

until her contact in Buenos Aires was exposed as a spy and fled the city. This led to a breakdown in her security plan because there was no pre-arranged danger signal to warn Velvalee that the spy was no longer in Buenos Aires. She continued sending her letters to her contact. But with no one there to accept the letters, the Argentine post office began to mark them "Return to Sender" and send them back to the United States.

Since Velvalee used her clients' return addresses, the letters were returned to women who had no idea who'd sent them, and the FBI (Federal Bureau of Investigation) was eventually called in. It didn't take long for them to focus their attention on Velvalee Dickinson. She was arrested at her doll shop in 1944. She was given the name "The Doll Woman" by the press, convicted of spying, and sent to prison for ten years.

2 Now do a test to see if your signal works. Use your danger signal in a message to a member of your network, asking her to meet you at a particular place. Does she pick up the danger signal and skip the meeting? If so, your safety check worked! If not, better review your security procedures!

MORE FROM HEADQUARTERS

You receive a message from a member of your spy network in **cipher**. When you decipher it, it reads like the letter shown above.

> Reporting as sceduled. I have checked out Building Alpha and found no signs of the enemy's presence. Will report on Building Delta next week. Will leave film at Drop Dead Nine.
>
> Jason

Do you see any danger signal here, or should you go ahead and pick up the film at Dead Drop Nine as usual? You can check your answer on page 48.

WHAT'S THE SECRET?

By using a danger signal, spies can protect their networks even while they themselves are in the hands of the enemy. But to make sure that counterspies don't catch on, it's important that the message sound as natural and normal as possible. If the message sounds strange, then the counterspies could suspect that it's a secret **code** and not send the message after all.

(continued from page 29)

At this point, you think the best bet would be to call your mom and give her the danger signal, alerting her that you and Dad are on your way home. You ask if you can borrow your dad's cell phone to call your mom to find out what's for dinner. Your dad hands over his phone, and you dial your home number.

"Hi, Mom," you say. "I'm starving. What's for dinner?"

"Gotcha," Mom says. "When will you be here?"

"Probably about ten minutes," you say.

Mom knows what to do next. She gathers all the guests who have arrived into the living room and sends your aunt down the street to meet the new arrivals to prevent them from spoiling the surprise.

You and Dad pull up to the house, which doesn't look unusual in any way. You chat with him about your upcoming soccer game and keep him occupied as he unlocks the front door. The two of you walk into the house and into the living room.

"SURPRISE!"

Dad jumps back, startled, and looks around in disbelief.

"Oh, my! How did you manage to do this?" he exclaims, laughing, as he gives you a big hug. You smile and look over at Mom, who gives you a thumbs up. Dad won't ever forget this birthday!

■ **Congratulations!**
Quest accomplished!

Yes!

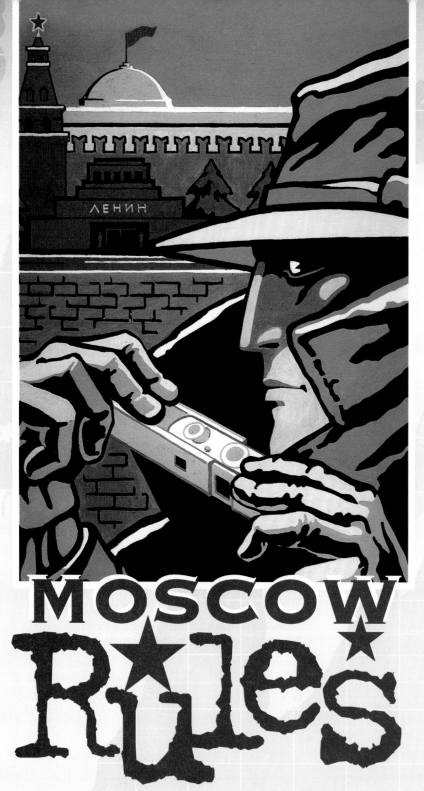

MOSCOW ★ Rules

For years during what was known as the Cold War (1945–1991), the United States and the former Soviet Union (which is now broken up into many smaller countries, including Russia) were locked in a chilling standoff. During this time, each country tried to outdo the other in every way it could, without actually going to war. The two countries competed at everything—from seeing which country could build more weapons to which one could win more medals at world athletic events. And in the middle of this icy relationship, two rival intelligence agencies, the American CIA and the Soviet KGB, worked desperately to stop the other's activities and to collect the other country's secrets at the same time.

The KGB had an extremely tough **counter-intelligence** service, which did everything you can imagine to watch, listen to, and follow anyone they suspected of spying in the Soviet Union. The Soviet intelligence agency worried about spies from all over the world, including Great Britain, West Germany, China, and, most of all, the United States. And they kept tabs on many of their own citizens, too, just in case they were collaborating with the enemy. With such a huge number of people to watch, the KGB ended up with so many surveillance teams that they were almost tripping over one another!

In Moscow, the capital city of the former Soviet Union, the KGB had a higher level of surveillance than anywhere else in the world. This made the job of CIA officers operating in

★ *Moscow*
The former Soviet Union

Moscow extremely difficult. So just how hard was it for CIA officers to get around?

To begin with, the U.S. embassy in Moscow (where many CIA officers secretly worked) was a target for Soviet electronic eavesdropping. The entire building was seeded with bugs to pick up conversations. Windows were bombarded with laser beams that could pick up vibrations caused by people talking inside and send those vibrations to KGB listening posts, where they were turned back into words! To counter these devices, U.S. officials had to create a secure area where they could discuss the most sensitive information. The area, nicknamed "The Bubble," was a clear plastic-walled box that was held off the room's floor with Plexiglas blocks. Since it was impossible to bug the Bubble, it was the *only* place in Moscow where CIA officers could freely talk!

The Moscow headquarters of the KGB's counterintelligence service.

A KGB badge.

The U.S. embassy in Moscow.

But before ever setting foot into the Bubble, or even in Moscow itself, all CIA officers were given a briefing that taught them the best way to operate around the KGB. And they were given a list of very specific orders to follow, which became known as the *Moscow Rules*. By following these rules of security, the CIA's spy operations in Moscow were able to stay up and running, despite the best efforts of the KGB to stop them.

The first and main Moscow Rule was that CIA officers were to assume that *every* Soviet person they met was part of the surveillance operation run by the KGB. That meant that the woman walking her dog on the street, the guy selling ice cream on the corner, even the hotel's cleaning woman could all be part of a larger KGB network. Most of the bartenders and half the taxi drivers in the city were assumed to be on the payroll of the KGB.

A KGB surveillance operation using concealed cameras.

The Soviets used all their resources to identify possible CIA officers in Moscow and then put them and their families under tight surveillance. Both the offices and the apartments of suspected CIA officers were bugged. In fact, the surveillance in Moscow was so complete that the officers often never had direct, face-to-face meetings with their contacts. This made it harder to do spy work in Moscow, but not impossible.

Another of the Moscow Rules involved the use of telephones—a risky way to communicate. All telephone lines going into the offices and apartments of foreigners were tapped and monitored by an army of eavesdroppers. The same was true of the phone lines of Soviet citizens who held jobs that put them in contact with sensitive information. To counter this, the CIA used one-way radio contact to deliver instructions to Soviets who were acting as spies for the United States. Instructions were broadcast in **cipher** from some location inside the Soviet Union or a neighboring country. Because the instructions were broadcast over a wide area and the receivers the spies used couldn't be

The KGB specialized in unusual ways of hiding cameras for surveillance. Here a camera is concealed behind a car's tail light. A rotating license plate made it easier to prevent the car from being detected by the target of the surveillance.

detected, this was a safe way to send messages to Soviet contacts.

Another important Moscow Rule warned CIA officers not to try to completely lose their surveillance teams. If a CIA officer made a "provocative move" (a move that would alarm the KGB) like suddenly running into a subway crowd or speeding away in an automobile, it would catch the KGB's attention, and they would step up their level of surveillance. In other words, if the surveillance team thought their target could lose them, they would move even closer, making communication with contacts and the use of **dead drops** that much more difficult.

Meanwhile, the KGB surveillance teams had plenty of reasons to do their jobs well. Members of the surveillance teams were punished if they lost track of a target for more than a few minutes. And if a target got away, the entire surveillance team got a pay cut and risked losing their Moscow apartments!

Knowing how hard KGB counterintelligence would work to watch them, CIA officers actually let surveillance teams remain relatively close, so that they would think they knew where their target was at all times. This way, an officer could slip the surveillance for a short period

to load or unload a dead drop without drawing suspicion.

As you can imagine, American intelligence officers certainly had a lot to think about in Moscow! Lucky for you, the Cold War is over, you don't operate in Moscow, *and* you don't have to go to the lengths that the CIA did to keep your **spy network** running smoothly. But, at the same time, many of the lessons learned during this era, and much of the wisdom found in the Moscow Rules, apply to spy security in general. So here are a few of the famous rules for you to reflect on and remember as you continue your spy work, wherever you are!

MOSCOW RULES

- ✪ Always listen to your gut; it is your operational antenna.
- ✪ Never go against your gut.
- ✪ Maintain a natural pace.
- ✪ Stay consistent over time.
- ✪ Know the opposition and their terrain intimately.
- ✪ Any operation can be aborted: If it feels wrong, then it is wrong.
- ✪ Keep your options open.

47

catch you later!

So, spy trainee, you should feel a bit more *secure* now that you've mastered all sorts of ways to keep yourself and your **spy network** safe. This month, you've beefed up security at your **base of operations** and made it a safer place to take care of spy business. Plus, you know some strategies for detecting surveillance while you're out and about on your missions. Not bad for a month's work!

Just remember that security doesn't automatically fall apart the moment you get into trouble. You just have to know *when* you're in trouble, and *what to do* to stop the trouble in its tracks.

Here's a final security challenge for you this month. If you received this message from a member of your network, what would you do? It's been written using the Caesar **cipher** that you learned in your *Trainee Handbook*. You can decode it by shifting the alphabet three letters. Once you know what the message says, you can decide what you should do! **(Check your answer below!)**

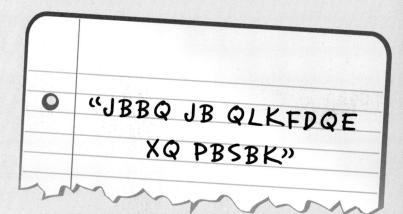

"JBBQ JB QLKFDQE XQ PBSBK"

theanswerspot